CONTAINER
GARDENING

ETHNE REUSS CLARKE

COLLINS

Products mentioned in this book

ICI Antkiller	contains	pirimiphos-methyl
Benlate* + 'Activex'	contains	benomyl
'Clean-Up'	contains	tar acids
'Sybol'	contains	pirimiphos-methyl

Products marked thus 'Sybol' are trade marks of Imperial Chemical Industries plc
Benlate* is a registered trade mark of Du Pont's
Read the label before you buy: use pesticides safely.

Editor Emma Johnson
Designers James Marks, Steve Wilson
Picture research Moira McIlroy

This edition first published 1988 by
William Collins Sons & Co Ltd
London · Glasgow · Sydney
Auckland · Toronto · Johannesburg

Reprinted 1989

British Library Cataloguing in Publication Data

Clark, Ethne Reuss
    Container gardening.——(Collins Aura garden handbooks).
    1. Container gardening
    I. Title
    635.9'86   SB418

ISBN 0–00–412375–1

Photoset by Bookworm Typesetting
Printed and bound in Hong Kong by Dai Nippon Printing
Company

Front cover: Container with fuchsias, lobelia, impatiens
Back cover: Container with lobelia, pelargoniums
Both by the Harry Smith Horticultural Photographic Collection

CONTENTS

INTRODUCTION

Mention the words 'container gar-den' and you conjure up images of an assortment of pots and tubs scattered randomly around the edges of a small concreted area. But container gardening offers much more than the chance to grow a few plants in a gardenless space. You can turn a barren space into a verdant Eden of secret cor-ners, sweet scents and rainbow col-ours. In containers it is possible to grow plants that require different soil conditions from those in the open garden, thus allowing the adventurous gardener plenty of scope.

With container gardening you can make use of different levels. Containers come in many shapes and sizes and pots and boxes can be fixed to walls to accommodate climbing and trailing plants.

There are few plants which cannot be grown in containers; mostly large trees and shrubs and rampant perennials that would look out of place anyway. With containers it is possible to have your herb garden growing just outside the kitchen door or, if you live in a flat, on the windowsill in a windowbox.

A container garden may require more attention than a conventional garden, both in planning and maintenance, but the reward is in the way the plants respond, with luxuriant growth and beautiful displays throughout the seasons.

Soil and drainage Since the plants are to be grown in a confined space, and for most of them the container will be their permanent home, it is essential to start out as you mean to carry on – providing the plants with the best possible conditions to stimulate healthy growth. The first step in this direction is to fill the containers with good soil. Unfortunately, many people, when faced with more than one or two containers, yield to the temptation of using soil dug from the garden to fill the tubs, thinking they will save money. They don't. Garden soil is bound to be full of weed seeds, may harbour a nasty fungus and lack many of the necessary nutrients essential for healthy growth. The gardener's time will be spent pulling weeds, combating disease and buying new plants to replace those that have died.

One of the alternatives is to purchase a proprietary potting compost such as John Innes No.3, which is a good general soil for containers,

but because it contains chalk it is not suitable for growing lime-haters such as azaleas. Also, it can prove expensive if you have a number of containers to fill.

Peat-based, soil-less composts are also presented as being suitable for container gardens, but they are really quite expensive and any food they contain is quickly used up by the plants. This means you must continuely feed the plants.

It is possible to mix together some soil-based and peat-based composts or you may wish to make your own potting compost from scratch; all the necessary ingredients are available from garden centres. The basic formula is 2 parts loam (weed-free soil) to 1 part peat and 1 part coarse sand or grit. This is measured by volume, so use an old bucket as a measure. The addition of a fertilizer such as Growmore or bonemeal would be beneficial: the amount to use is dependent upon the amount of com-

post you are making. Otherwise, if it is available, add well-rotted manure or 'Forest Bark' Ground and Composted to the above recipe.

Do the mixing with a small spade in a clean corner of the patio or another paved area. Work against a wall so that the soil doesn't scatter

Containers can be used to create a garden on paved patios (bottom) or to turn the front of a house into a garden (below left). One attractive pot can become the focal point (below).

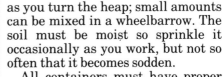

as you turn the heap; small amounts can be mixed in a wheelbarrow. The soil must be moist so sprinkle it occasionally as you work, but not so often that it becomes sodden.

All containers must have proper drainage. Without it the soil would become waterlogged and sour and the plant roots would soon rot. But it is not enough to have a few holes in the bottom of the container. You must cover these with a layer of crocks (broken pots), and in containers that are more than 25cm (10in) deep, the crocks must be covered with a 2.5cm (1in) deep layer of gravel; the size used in fish tanks is ideal. Without these layers of crocks and gravel, the soil would drain too quickly and wash out of the container each time it was watered.

Additionally, some plants, such as lilies, will not tolerate damp conditions, so an additional layer of sharp sand or fine grit over the gravel ensures proper drainage.

WINDOWBOXES

This is the most common type of container for plants, and there are few windows that will not accommodate a box. Windowboxes are available in many sizes and in a range of materials, from plastic to terracotta.

The size of box you choose will depend on the size of the windowsill, but it should not overhang the sill. Ideally, it should be 2.5cm (1in) shallower than the depth of the sill, at least 20cm (8in) deep to provide adequate room for the plants' root systems, and long enough to fit comfortably within the space.

On casement type windows that open outwards, the box can be placed below the sill rather than resting on it, so it should be only half as wide again as the sill overhang. To have exactly the desired size of windowbox, it is easiest to make your own, (see page 9). Use any type of timber as long as it is 2.5cm (1in) thick. Teak, pine and split logs can be used; teak can be stained to give a rich effect, pine can be painted (but choose the colour carefully), and split logs give a rustic effect.

Use water resistant glue, and make sure screws and nails will not rust. The interior of the box must be treated to prevent rot, and there are wood preservatives available which will not harm plants. Don't forget to drill drainage holes in the base of the box.

Windowsills always slant forward to allow water to drain away. Therefore, you must put wedges under the front edge of the box to keep it level. This will also aid drainage. It is best if the wedges are fixed to the bottom of the box. If the box is to rest on an overhead sill it is essential for safety that it is fixed to the wall or secured to the sill. L-brackets fixed to the ends of the box and the wall are probably the easiest way of doing this.

Also, use a drip tray on overhead boxes to prevent accidents.

Boxes fixed under sills should be placed on trays. Put a layer of gravel in the tray to lift the bottom of the box out of the water that has collected. Use L-brackets to support the box and attach it to the wall by screwing the back to the brickwork.

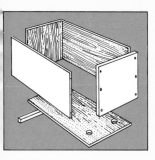

1. An exploded view of a windowbox; the end pieces fit within the front and back pieces.

2. Use L-brackets to secure the box to the wall.

3. Under sill boxes should also be supported with L-brackets; the drip tray should be 2-3cm (¾-1in) below the box base.

Planting the windowbox Put a layer of crocks and gravel in the bottom of the box and then fill to within 5cm (2in) of the top with compost. Plant up with your chosen scheme and then fill in around the plants with compost to within 2.5cm (1in) of the top of the box. Water the plants well and add more compost if necessary.

Bulbs and dwarf evergreens are lovely companions for permanent display, but most other perennials are too large for windowbox cultivation. Probably the most popular combination for boxes is one of trail- ing ivy, or the grey-leaved perennial *Ballota pseudodictamnus*, and annuals such as petunias, pansies, lobelia and geraniums. By replacing the annuals as they die off, a long floral display can be achieved. Windowboxes are ideal places to grow scented plants; a small breeze across a windowbox by an open window will fill the room with fragrance. Try heliotrope and sweet alyssum and the dwarf strains of nicotiana.

To create the best effect windowboxes should be closely planted. This means that they soon fill with roots, which in turn means the soil dries out more quickly, and the available food is soon used. So pay particular attention to watering, and water in a liquid feed (such as ICI Liquid Growmore) at least once a week.

Some container gardeners fill their windowboxes with peat or horticultural vermiculite and plunge pot-grown plants into this, rather than plant them directly into the box. This makes it easier to change planting schemes as the season progresses and plants go out of flower. If a plant becomes diseased, it can be removed without harming the surrounding plants or disturbing their roots.

Windowboxes are popular containers and can be planted for permanent display | with ivies and evergreens (below), or with annuals for summer colour (left).

HANGING BASKETS

Ready-made hanging baskets are available in plastic-coated wire (usually green in colour) and also as plastic bowls complete with attached drip tray. Wire baskets allow more scope for planting as plants can be grown through the mesh and the entire surface of the basket can be used as growing space.

Plastic bowls are easier to tend because they retain water better than the wire baskets, but their colour and shiny surface do not necessarily enhance the plants they contain.

Baskets can be suspended from the cross beams of pergolas, porch roofs, from brackets against walls, and just about anywhere you can fix a hook or bracket. However, make sure that when the basket is in position, it does not impede progress through or around the space in which it is hanging. Make absolutely certain that the support is secure and strong enough to take the considerable weight of a full basket.

Planting a basket Obviously you can't fill a wire basket with compost; it must be contained within the mesh and there are three ways of doing this. Sphagnum moss, available in bags from garden centres, can be used to line the basket. It has a pleasing, natural appearance; the disadvantage is that although it is dense enough to contain the growing medium, it is porous and dries out fairly quickly. Green plastic sheeting is an alternative lining, but it is unsightly and must have holes poked through to provide drainage.

The best lining is a combination of both. First, line the basket with the moss; be generous and don't leave gaps. Next, cover the moss lining

1. Line the basket with moss and a sheet of polythene. Add some compost.

2. Plant the outside of the basket, putting plants through moss and plastic. Add more compost.

3. Plant the top of the basket, filling with compost to within 5cm (2in) of the rim.

with a sheet of black or green plastic. The basket can now be filled with compost. Because baskets dry out more quickly than other containers, add more peat to the compost to make it moisture retentive.

If you are going to plant only the upper surface of the basket, fill to within 5cm (2in) of the top. Then use a skewer to poke drainage holes in the plastic, working through the mesh of the basket.

If you plan to plant all over the basket's surface, put some compost in the plastic and gently ease the roots of the plants through the moss and the slits. Add more compost and put in more plants until the basket is finished. Position upright subjects in the centre of the basket, pendulous plants around the outer edge. Bowls are planted as for windowboxes, with crocks and gravel for base drainage. Small annuals, ivy, and any smaller plants with a trailing or pendulous habit, are suitable for basket growing. Fuchsias are particularly good.

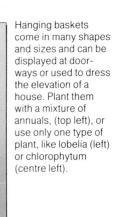

Hanging baskets come in many shapes and sizes and can be displayed at doorways or used to dress the elevation of a house. Plant them with a mixture of annuals, (top left), or use only one type of plant, like lobelia (left) or chlorophytum (centre left).

TUBS AND TERRACOTTA

Because of their size, tubs and troughs offer more opportunities for growing a wider range of plants and for exploring the potential of container gardening. Provided they are treated carefully, tubs and troughs are very durable.

Tubs Today, the most common type of tub seen in gardens is the wooden half-barrel. These are available either purpose-made for planting or as whisky-barrels that have been sawn in half. The former come in a range of sizes, treated and finished to withstand the elements. Compared to whisky barrels, they are more expensive.

Whisky barrels or casks require a small amount of preparation before they can be planted. Usually all this amounts to is drilling drainage holes in the bottom. The inside of a whisky cask will have been charred, so further treatment with wood preservatives is not necessary. The exterior will be a satisfying dark brown, but you can give it several coats of wood stain to deepen the shade, and give it a 'newer' appearance. Half-barrels can be treated as if they were nothing more than raised sections of the open garden; in them you can grow small trees, shrubs and perennials in colourful informal groupings.

Another type of wooden container is the Versailles tub. This is a square box, rather formal in appearance and usually painted white. For this reason it is best to plant formally using a clipped bay or box as a central feature, or perhaps a fruit tree or standard rose. A pair of Versailles tubs, identically planted and placed at each side of a doorway, or to emphasize the axis of a garden plan, is most effective.

Planting Tubs usually contain some permanent planting and for this reason the initial preparation

Trees and shrubs used for permanent planting enjoy the space of wooden half barrels (left). Square

Versailles tubs look best with a formal planting, such as a pair of clipped bay trees (below).

must be done carefully to ensure that drainage is adequate and the soil clean and rich.

If you have to drill drainage holes, use a large drill bit so that the holes are at least 1.5cm (½in) in diameter. Drill 7 or 9 holes, evenly spaced on the bottom of the barrel. Now put the barrel in its position; the site must not be one that is sun-baked or you'll be endlessly watering, and it should not be constantly buffeted by cold winds, which would retard the plants' growth. Raise the barrel off the ground by standing it on three bricks. This is essential; it will aid drainage and also deter pests.

Now is also the time to consider whether you will want to move the barrel around, because once it is full of soil and plants it will be extremely difficult to shift. Casters attached to pieces of wood, which are in turn attached to the bottom of the barrel, will make moving easier. Use three casters so that the barrel will be less likely to wobble on uneven ground. Have ready a quantity of crocks, large and small, gravel, peat and the prepared compost.

Put the largest crocks in first, placing them over, but not plugging, the drainage holes. Carefully fill in between these with the smaller crocks so that the bottom of the barrel is covered. Next put a layer of gravel and pat it down gently to make an even surface over the crocks. Cover the gravel with a 5cm (2in) layer of peat, breaking up any lumps you come across. Fill the barrel with compost to within 10cm (4in) of the top. After the barrel has been planted, add more compost to bring the level up to within 5cm (2in) of the top.

Planting schemes As mentioned before, tubs allow the container gardener more scope. You can plant

tubs permanently using small trees and shrubs, but try to use evergreens if possible as the bare branches of a deciduous tree have a curiously dead, impoverished look and it is important to avoid this with container gardening. If you are planting more than one container, decide upon some unifying element, just as you would in the open garden. This can be either colour, (planting flowers predominantly of one shade or using complementary colours); form (a plant with upright habit in each barrel); or contrast (playing foliage shapes off against each other, or dark against light). If you are planting bulbs, these should be put in after all the other plants are in place, otherwise you would be likely to dig them up or stab them with the trowel.

Terracotta Containers made of unglazed terracotta are certainly among the most satisfying, as the warm reddish brown of the clay is a perfect complement to the subtle green shades of foliage; it is also a good foil to most flower tints.

The range of sizes and styles that terracotta containers are available

in is extensive, from the simplest flowerpot shape to elaborately moulded urns based on styles popular in gardens of the Italian Renaissance. Thus the mood of your garden can be established by the style of containers used.

Planting Drainage holes in terracotta pots will be either one large hole in the centre of the base or several around the perimeter. These must be covered with crocks and, in the case of large pots, gravel and peat, as for the half-barrel. With single drainage holes, make sure the crocks don't create a plug; a large curved piece placed with the convex side facing will prevent this happening. Put large pots in position before filling and, as with half-barrels, put bricks underneath to raise them off the ground.

Dishes for pots to stand in are available in various sizes. This is an advantage if you wish to contain the water, but as most plants don't like standing in water, any that collects will have to be poured off – a difficult task with large containers.

There are many different types of plant container – from the large terracotta pot, which has a sculptural quality, to the elegant stone urn or basic wooden tub. The containers and plants look effective either grouped together or on their own.

Algae and moss can grow on terracotta, so from time to time it will be necessary to scrub the exterior of the containers to keep them clean. Terracotta is also porous. This means that during hot weather the moisture in the soil is likely to evaporate quite quickly. Consequently, you must pay greater attention to keeping the plants well-watered; once a day during dry spells should be enough. Water during the early evening when the sun is low so that the water won't evaporate as soon as you apply it.

Other materials Tubs are available in plastic, cast concrete, and moulded fibreglass. The chief advantage of containers made in these materials is their durability, the main disadvantage is their appearance – shiny white plastic, turquoise blue concrete and the dead grey tinge of most fibreglass garden ornaments is singularly unappealing. Also, containers at the lower end of the market will inevitably be less well-made, and a large-size tub full of soil and well-stocked with plants could gradually distort under the weight, or even crack as the root systems increase in size.

This is not to say that all containers made of man-made materials are a bad choice. Genuine antique lead cisterns are scarce and seventeenth century carved stone urns are expensive, but convincing man-made replicas are available. They may cost a little more, but if the effect of antique splendour is what you are after it is worth the expense. Modern designs for containers can be unusual and add a note of humour to the garden. Stacking towers, intended for strawberry cultivation, work equally well when planted up with trailing plants, or those with pendulous flowers.

SINKS AND TROUGHS

For those gardeners wishing to specialise in the cultivation of dwarf plants, alpine or otherwise, old-fashioned stone sinks or farmyard troughs are the preferred containers. In the open garden, or planted in containers with other larger plants, diminutive alpine beauties are soon overshadowed. But on their own they excel and can even be provided with a micro-landscape as a perfect setting.

Ten or twenty years ago these sinks and troughs were relatively easy to come by, but today they are rare. On the other hand, porcelain sinks are more readily available as the trend for house modernisation advances through the country's kitchens. These cumbersome white monoliths can be found in builders yards and skips, and can usually be had for the taking. The sinks can, of course, be left as they are, but it is far better to cover them in the following manner; the result looks remarkably like stone.

Using a bucket as a measure, mix together 1 part ready-mix cement, 1½ parts peat, 2 parts sand. Turn it over several times until it is well-combined. Add just enough water to the mixture to make a stiff paste. Next clean the sink well to remove any trace of dirt or grease and prop it off the ground on bricks. Paint over the exterior surface, and

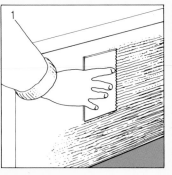

Old, unused porcelain sinks can be disguised to resemble stone troughs. After cleaning, coat with a mixture of concrete and peat (1). Then apply a coating of glue and stone mix. Apply it roughly and remember to carry it over the edges to enhance the deception (2).

the interior about 10cm (4in) down each side, with a general purpose contact adhesive, such as Unibond. When this is tacky, put on a pair of rubber gloves and begin to smear the cement and peat mixture over the glued surfaces of the sink. Cover it with a layer about 1.5cm (½in) thick. Don't smooth it over but leave

Stone troughs are ideally suited to the creation of miniature gardens, using dwarf alpines and evergreens, which like the good drainage and appear natural in the setting of stone and pebble.

the surface slightly bumpy so that it resembles stone.

Leave the sink to dry for at least five hours, then mix some compost, manure and milk in a small bowl. It should be fairly liquid for painting onto the 'stone' surfaces; it will encourage the growth of mosses and lichens to complete the deception.

Planting Put the sink in its chosen site; an open, airy position is best. Place the sink on three bricks to lift it off the ground. If the plug hole is at one end, raise the opposite end slightly higher to ensure good drainage. Cover the drainage hole with a large crock and then spread a layer of gravel about 1cm (⅓in) deep in the sink bottom.

Many of the alpines prefer a loose soil so the compost you use should consist of equal parts leaf-mould, sharp sand and loam. A collection of several sinks, each with a different type of soil, from acid peaty soil to a limy alkaline one, would enable you to grow a wide variety of unusual alpines that could not otherwise be grown in your garden. Since these plants don't require regular applications of fertilizer, it is beneficial to add a small amount of 'Forest Bark' Ground and Composted to the planting mixture.

To give the sink garden the look of a micro-landscape, add a few attractive rocks of various sizes. They should be large enough to be partially buried without taking up all the planting space. Plants that are especially fussy about drainage will appreciate being sited next to these rocks. When you have finished planting, scatter a thin layer of small chippings of granite or limestone over the soil surface for lime-loving plants. This will help to retain moisture as well as enhance the appearance of the tiny garden.

RAISED BEDS

While some gardeners may choose to make a container garden because they don't have access to a conventional garden, there are people who are unable to realise their dream garden because they are confined to a wheelchair or have a disability that restricts their movement. This is an area where containers are particularly welcome.

Raised beds are nothing more than outsize windowboxes and tubs. They are usually made from bricks or old railway sleepers. Logs, used sideways or upright, can also make the retaining walls for raised beds.

Planning Because raised beds are 'architectural', they do require careful planning, and there are several important elements to keep in mind. The beds should be sited near the house or be within easy reach. The height of the retaining walls must be only as high as is convenient for the gardener to work the top of the bed. The width must not be greater than the distance the gardener can comfortably stretch. If the bed can be worked from all sides, then the gardener should be able to easily reach the middle of the bed.

The beds must be sited so that a person in a wheelchair can manoeuvre around and between them. The walkways between the beds must be even, firm and, if paved, a non-slip surface should be used. Gardeners always have tools, and places must be provided around the beds for tools to be laid down. Water must be easily available and an outdoor tap and lightweight garden hose should be nearby. All this may sound complicated, but it is better to design the garden properly, than to go to the expense of building it and then find it unsuitable.

LEFT Raised beds give handicapped gardeners the chance to create beautiful gardens, as plants and soil are brought within easy reach.

ABOVE Collections of dwarf or low-growing plants are ideal subjects for raised beds. A miniature rose collection makes a lovely border.

Planting It is not necessary to fill the raised bed completely with soil. If you were to do this, the moisture from the soil would seep through and discolour the walls of the bed. Fill it about two-thirds full with rubble and tamp this down so that it will not shift or settle too much when the soil and plants are put in.

It is necessary to put a barrier over the rubble to prevent the soil being washed down. Turves of grass, laid with the soil-side facing and placed closely together over the rubble, is most satisfactory. Over this, lay a thick layer of newspaper – don't unfold the sheets, lay them down as they come. Newspaper is a good mulch and retains water well. Give the beds a good soaking before you infill with compost.

As with all containers, the type of soil you use depends upon the type of plants you wish to grow. The soil will settle, so do not plant for a week or two, then you can top up the level as necessary. If you have used wooden logs, the gaps between the logs can be planted with small-growing wall plants; this will look pretty and help to retain the soil. Pieces of peat brick, packed into the gaps here and there, will allow you to grow a wider variety of plants.

Don't forget that wood must be treated with a preservative to keep out pests and fungus disease. Use one that will not affect the plants.

Planting raised beds Tall plants should be excluded from raised beds as the effect is rather like putting giants on stilts. Make your selection from the low-growing shrubs of compact habit, and use some of the trailing plants to clothe the front of the beds (without obscuring any of the wall plants).

Apart from these strictures, use the raised bed as you would the open garden. Underplant shrubs with spring flowering bulbs, create small herbaceous borders, plant one bed as a herb garden. Most plants will thrive in well-drained conditions.

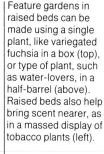

Feature gardens in raised beds can be made using a single plant, like variegated fuchsia in a box (top), or type of plant, such as water-lovers, in a half-barrel (above). Raised beds also help bring scent nearer, as in a massed display of tobacco plants (left).

Raised water gardens Because of the solid construction of a brick raised bed, artificial pond gardens can be created. Use one of the fibreglass pond forms – preferably not aquamarine – and build a low raised bed around it, catching the edge of the pond form on the inner wall.

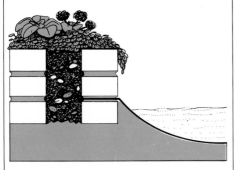

The retaining walls of a raised bed allow an artifical pond to be incorporated (below).

The pond form is caught in the mortar and plants can be grown in between (above).

Fill the pond three-quarters full with large gravel or pebbles (a trip to the seashore should provide you with all you need, but wash them well to remove all traces of salt). Plant moisture-loving plants all around the edges of the pond, and in the pond itself use those plants that grow naturally in water.

If the plants you obtain have soil around the roots, wash it away and put the bare roots directly into the pebbles, the weight will anchor the plants in position. Water lilies are the most elegant water plants to grow, and dwarf species like *Nymphaea odorata minor* or *N. pygmea alba* can be planted in terracotta pots and then put among the pebbles. Keep an eye on the water level and top it up with rain water, which is free of chemicals that might be detrimental; otherwise use tap water. Feed with a general liquid fertilizer like ICI Liquid Growmore.

PATIO CONTAINERS

Heavy-duty plastic bags full of prepared compost are deservedly popular for patio gardening. Growing bags contain a peat-based compost blended with essential plant nutrients for growing excellent vegetables. Many flowers and herbs will also thrive in the conditions these easily portable containers provide.

Although the bags can be simply laid upon the ground, it is more attractive to put them in something, like a framework of logs or even a low retaining wall of stacked bricks. Placed against a wall or trellis, climbing plants can be grown and trained neatly.

Miscellaneous containers Large bowls from old-fashioned washstand sets can also be used as containers, as can chamber-pots, coal scuttles, chimney-pots, buckets, stoneware jars and many other similar types of container. Such containers will not have drainage holes, nor will it be possible to drill the holes. The exceptions to this are chimney-pots that have an open bottom, and metal buckets that can have holes punched in the bottom. Drainage can be provided by using a deep layer of crocks and gravel. Use a loose soil mixture; one that is largely grit is ideal for a cactus garden, fibrous peat is good for bulbs.

Chimney-pots can be used like plant stands, and potted plants fitted into the tops. Metal containers should be lined with heavy plastic to retard corrosion. With a little imagination, much of what is discarded as rubbish can be turned into planters. Packing cases, tea chests and other wooden crates can be used. They must be treated with wood preservative, and if there are large gaps between the slats of wood, these must be filled. You can use them as a frame-work and cover the

exterior with split larch poles.

Worn-out car tyres are popular as they are inexpensive, water-resistant and can be stacked to the desired height. Don't be tempted to paint the tyres white, the paint inevitably discolours and in the end looks unpleasantly shabby. Tractor tyres can be used to make large container gardens.

However imaginative you think containers such as the ones just described may be, remember that they are there to provide a setting for plants and therefore must not detract from the beauty of the flowers by being either curious or unattractive.

Growing bags and chimney pots are just a few of the containers suitable for patio gardens, but take care that the plants don't have to fight the pots for attention.

CHOOSING PLANTS

Container gardens offer the keen gardener a chance to grow whatever he or she wishes with increased chances of success. This is because the soil conditions in a properly prepared tub or windowbox will be ideal for healthy plant growth.

Because the soil can be suited to the type of plant, the gardener can grow subjects which require soil of a type totally unlike that in the garden; perfect drainage can be provided for plants which require such situations, or heavy moist soils can be used to grow plants which need constant moisture at their roots. But the main attraction is simply that containers provide an opportunity to garden where you might not otherwise be able to. A paved forecourt in front of a house can be a barren and unwelcoming sight. Add a few barrels full of scented flowers and the whole appearance changes.

Decide on a theme Before you plant, give some thought to the effect you wish to achieve: do you want year round colour or a vibrant splash in summer only; do you want a formal or informal arrangement? What situation will the plants be growing in? Are the containers in partial shade or full sun? Do they face east, west, north or south? Answer these questions and choose the plants accordingly.

Careful thought should be given to colour and form as well as choice of plant. Trailing geraniums and pendant fuchsias (far top left) reflect each other in colour and habit; collection of evergreen plants (left) makes a permanent show in subtle shades of green; hanging baskets carry the garden bedding up the side of a house (far bottom left), all demonstrating the success achieved through good planning.

AFTERCARE

As with any garden, the plants must be nourished, watered, kept tidy and protected from pests and diseases. Water regularly, particularly in dry hot weather; during the growing season this may mean every day.

Make sure that the soil is completely moistened, and that the outside of each container (other than those made of plastic) is thoroughly wetted. Soil, and the ·nutrients it contains, will be washed out by the watering and must be replaced. Liquid feeds are the handiest to use because they can be regularly given with routine watering. ICI Liquid Growmore provides all the necessary nutrients for healthy growth; for windowboxes and hanging baskets try 'Kerispikes', little fingers of fertilizer that release the nutrients as the containers are watered. Each autumn it is necessary to top up the

Feed container plants regularly; 'Kerispikes' are helpful in this as several spikes placed in the tub release the food over a period of weeks. Renew them as necessary.

Keep containers tidy at all times. Dead-head regularly (1), and water frequently (2) as soil in containers does dry out quickly.

soil level, adding fresh compost. Every three years all the soil should be removed and replaced with new compost.

The outsides of terracotta pots and wooden tubs should be cleaned periodically to remove mosses and lichens; use a general garden cleanser such as 'Clean-up'. On the other hand, the appearance of stone, cast concrete and so on will improve with a discreet layer of these tiny plants.

Keep a sharp eye open for snails and slugs; they nestle along the inner edges of tubs under overhanging foliage and live happy well-fed lives unless removed. Use a slug-killer to be sure of destroying the tiny black slugs that live just below the surface of the soil.

Earthworms and ants attack the root system of container-grown plants and top-growth will appear wilted. Watch for earthworm casts on the soil surface and at the first sign water in a suitable earthworm killer. Ants can get into the tubs through the drainage holes. Small piles of finely textured soil at the base or under the tubs is a sign of infestation; ICI Antkiller puffed under and around the container will help, otherwise use a liquid drench of 'Sybol'.

Aphids, mildew, whitefly and other garden pests and diseases will spread quickly through the close confines of a container garden. Therefore, begin a programme of regular spraying early in the growing season, using a preparation such as 'Sybol' for the insects, and Benlate + 'Activex' for the fungal diseases. In gardening, an ounce of prevention is far more valuable than a pound of cure.

Once you have established healthy plants in ideal growing conditions, you must help them to keep up appearances. Nothing looks uglier than container gardens full of dead annual plants, dropped leaves, unpruned trees, and ragged shrubs that should have been clipped after flowering. Dead-head all annuals – it keeps them neat and prolongs the flowering. Cut out all diseased and dying branches on plants, and trim and tidy whenever necessary. Shabbiness is so much more noticeable in a small garden.

SIXTY OF THE BEST

The following plants listed in categories have been chosen because they are suitable for containers.

ANNUALS

These are plants that complete the growing cycle in one season. Some are classed as hardy, which means they withstand frost so can be planted out earlier in the season than those that are termed half-hardy. Half-hardy annuals are not frost-resistant, so can't be planted out until danger of frost is past. Annuals are easily raised from seed, and hardy types may be sown in flowering positions early in the spring and then thinned to allow room for proper growth. Alternatively, grow them in seed trays under glass, then harden off gradually before planting out. Half-hardy types should be treated in this way. Many annuals will self-sow, so watch for seedlings and transplant thinnings to increase stocks.

Biennials are plants that complete the growing cycle over two years; seed is sown and germinated in one year, and the plant produces its flowers the following year. So unless you have space in the garden to raise biennials to flowering, it is best to buy nursery-grown plants. Most annuals and biennials require full sun and well-drained soil.
H = Hardy; HH = Half-hardy;
B = Biennial

Alyssum

ALYSSUM (H)
Sweet-smelling tufts of tiny flowers, attractive to bees. Use at the front of windowboxes or as an edging around the rim of a barrel. Self-sows. Height up to 10cm (4in), plant 20 cm (8in) apart.

ANTIRRHINUM (HH)
Multi-coloured snapdragons are old favourites. Pinch out the growing tips of each plant to encourage bushiness. There are dwarf strains available, growing little more than 20cm (8in) tall, but the taller growing varieties are the most useful in containers. Choose a rust-resistant strain. Plant out 20-30cm (8-12in) apart.

BEGONIA (HH)
Fleshy little flowers with stiff heart-shaped leaves, they make attractive clumps about 15cm (6in) high, with a similar spread. Begonias are good for colour later in the season. Quite difficult to raise from seed, so purchase nursery-grown plants.

BELLIS (B)
Low-growing, daisy-flowered in shades of red to pink. Neat, bushy habit, roughly 16cm (6¼in) high. Plant 15cm (6in) apart at the front of the container.

DIANTHUS BARBATUS (B)
Old cottage garden Sweet William, sweetly scented of cloves, in shades from deep crimson to palest pink. About 45cm (1½ft) tall, so use in the centre of containers, or fill windowboxes so the perfume can waft into the room. Plant out at least 20cm (8in) apart.

Main picture: Begonia *semperflorens* Top left: Bellis 'Pomponette' Top right: Dianthus *barbatus*

HELIOTROPE (HH)

One of the best flower perfumes, heliotope is a must for windowboxes. The colour of flower and foliage is also attractive. Grows to about 25cm (10in), plant 20cm (8in) apart. Seed germinates unevenly or not at all, so look for nursery-grown plants.

IMPATIENS (HH)

Commonly known as Busy Lizzie, they are remarkably good value for money, making masses of flowers over a long season. They will do well in shade or sun, but be sure not to plant out too early as they are very frost tender. Impatiens are not easy to raise, so buy nursery-grown plants.

LOBELIA (HH)

Wonderful trailing plants for the front of windowboxes, tubs and hanging baskets. Upright-growing varieties are also available so take care when purchasing seed or plants. Plant about 15cm (6in) apart.

NICOTIANA (HH)

Sweet smelling tobacco plants are ideal container subjects. The flowers of most varieties open only in the evening, unless planted in shade. Use the white or lime green flowered types for special colour effects. For windowboxes be sure to buy dwarf varieties; taller growing types can be used in large tubs.

Heliotrope

Impatiens sultanii

Lobelia

Petunia 'Prelude Velvet'

Viola

PANSY AND VIOLA (H)

Multi-coloured flowers, produced over a long season, make the pansy a favourite container-garden flower. Most garden centres stock the large-flowered Pacific Hybrids, but the petals on these are so huge that the flowerheads often flop over and the beauty is lost. Since pansies are so easy to grow from seed (sown early in spring to flower that summer), you can be selective and raise some of the smaller-flowered, more compact violas in a wide range of subtle tints. Pansies and violas seed themselves readily.

PETUNIA (HH)

Another container classic, popular for its trumpet-shaped flowers in a wide range of colours, and for its long flowering period. There are two basic types: Multiflora which form bushy plants with small but plentiful flowers, and Grandiflora, the large-flowered varieties. Unless they will be growing in a sheltered spot, choose a type bred for weather resistance.

33

PERENNIALS

These are plants that live for several years, flowering and increasing in size over the seasons. Herbaceous perennials die down completely each autumn and start into growth the following spring. Some perennials are evergreen, others rather shrub-like, such as pelargoniums and fuchsias. Use perennials where a permanent planting is required, but remember that most will have to be lifted and divided every three years to maintain healthy plants. Lifting and planting should be done in the autumn or early spring before the plants have started into growth.

ANEMONE PULSATILLA
Clump-forming plants producing quantities of star-shaped flowers in early spring. Height up to 25cm (10in).

AQUILEGIA
Multicoloured, trumpet-shaped flowers with a graceful upright habit and pretty foliage. Height to 45cm (1½ft).

BERGENIA
Large round leaves and clusters of pink flowers early in the year. Low-growing, clump-forming. Height to 25cm (10in).

DIANTHUS DELTOIDES
Plants form a mat of deep reddish green foliage from which spring upright stems carrying tiny crimson flowers throughout the summer. Height to 15cm (6in).

HELIANTHEMUM
Low-growing, with grey leaves or dark green foliage, covered in tiny flowers all summer. These plants prefer dry conditions. Height up to 15cm (6in).

Aquilegia

Bergenia

Dianthus deltoides

Helianthemum

IBERIS SEMPERVIRENS
Evergreen mounds of glossy green foliage covered over with clusters of white flowers from spring until midsummer. Height to 20cm (8in).

PELARGONIUMS
Popularly known as geraniums, they are available in a wide range of colours and leaf form. They are not hardy so should be lifted and overwintered in a cool greenhouse. Alternatively, take cuttings in autumn after flowering.

POLYANTHUS
More colourful member of the primula family providing flowers through winter into spring. Good partners for spring bulbs.

Inset: *Iberis sempervirens*   *Pelargonium domesticum*

BULBS, CORMS AND TUBERS

There are few plants that belong in this section which will not do well in containers; in fact, some will do much better than they would in the open garden, as it is easier to provide perfect conditions for growth. Bulbs in containers should be planted a little deeper than is usual and they should be put in after any permanent herbaceous plants or shrubs. Then you do not risk damaging them.

Here are just a few of the bulbous plants that can be grown in containers, and many beautiful effects can be achieved using others, such as tulips, hyacinths, freesias, crocuses and so on.

Cyclamen hederifolium

CYCLAMEN
Cyclamen coum, C. hederifolium, and *C.purpurescens* are all desirable hardy cyclamen for containers. Some strains of *C.persicum* are good winter-flowering pot plants. They should be grown as individual specimens so that their dainty flowers and perfume can be easily appreciated.

DAFFODILS AND NARCISSI
Be adventurous and choose some of the species or less common hybrids such as:
N.canaliculatus Height up to 10cm (4in), 3-4 small, perfumed flowers to each stem.
N.bulbocodium Height up to 10cm (4in), the shape of the clear yellow flowers give it the common name 'Hoop Petticoat'.
N.jonquilla 'Baby Moon'. Height up to 30cm (1ft), pale yellow sweet scent. Also good is *N.j.* 'Trevithian'.
N.triandrus 'Thalia'. Height up to 30cm (1ft), pure white, sweet scented flower clusters.

Narcissus 'Fortune'

Iris histrioides 'Major'

Iris danfordiae

Iris reticulata

IRIS

Iris histrioides, I.reticulata and *I.danfordiae*. Height 10-15cm (4-6in), are bulbous irises suitable for these boxes and troughs. *I.graminea*, height 15-20cm (6-8in), grows from thread-like roots and flowers very early in spring. The dainty blooms, smelling of ripe plums, are often hidden by the leaves.

LILIES

These beautiful flowers are often difficult to grow successfully in the open garden as most require perfectly drained, rich soil, the exception to this being *Lilium candidum*, the Madonna Lily, which likes to be shallowly planted in coarse soil in full sun. A container will provide these conditions.

Plant lilies of one variety in deep clay pots, five bulbs to a 30cm (1ft) pot. Put a layer of crocks in the bottom of the pot, cover with 5-7cm (2-2½in) of compost and then a 2cm (¾in) layer of grit or sand to ensure perfect drainage. Place the bulbs on top of the grit, carefully spreading out the roots, and position three bamboo canes between the bulbs to

Lilium candidum

serve as supports; use tall canes, as lilies can reach great heights – *L.regale* can grow up to 2m (6½ ft). Plant lilies in November, making sure that the bulbs you buy are fresh; avoid bulbs that feel flaccid and have withered roots. Don't delay planting, if you can help it. If you have to wait, plunge the bulbs into moist peat to await planting.

LILY OF THE VALLEY

Convallaria majalis. A good choice for windowboxes, but plant them on their own and then move the box to a shaded part of the garden after flowering so that the leaves can be left to die back naturally.

Lilium regale

Lily of the Valley

HERBS

Pots of herbs kept near the kitchen are a valuable addition to any cook's *batterie de cuisine.* Windowboxes of chives, tarragon, and parsley, tubs of shrubby herbs such as sage, rosemary, thyme and bay are as attractive as they are useful.

Mint is particularly well-suited to container growing; in the open garden it can be troublesome, spreading rapidly by means of a sturdy creeping root system, and unless contained, taking over large chunks of flower border. But planted in troughs or tubs, you can easily grow several varieties of mint: Bowles apple mint with large round 'furry' leaves is especially desirable. It has a sweeter, softer flavour than the familiar spearmint. Some herb plants are valued more for their decorative habit than culinary purposes. Feathery-leaved dill and fennel (particularly bronze-leaved fennel) and the stately angelica, can be used as part of a garden scheme, contributing only the occasional branch for flavouring.

Bay trees score high in both areas; we are all familiar with the flavour of the leaves and the sight of a pair of bay trees neatly clipped into the shape of pyramids, cones, ball-shaped standards and so on, residing in neat tubs either side of an entrance. The formality of this display can be enhanced with herbs by underplanting (in a large enough tub) to form a pattern of leaf and colour.

Herbs appreciate a warm, sunny position, well away from cold winds, and any good soil will do as long as it is well drained. The exception to this is mint which prefers cool, moist soil in partial shade. Parsley pots are specially designed for herb-growing, having a number of lipped 'pockets'

Basil

around the sides in which the herbs may be planted. This is an excellent way to grow a number of different herbs where space is severely restricted. Here is a list of some of the herbs you shouldn't be without.

ANGELICA
Perennial, reaching 2m (6½ft) in one season. The stems smell like gin when crushed; chop up a few pieces and add to stewed fruit or crystallize by boiling in sugar and water.

BASIL
Annual. Sow seed under glass in late spring and plant out when all danger of frost is past. Pungent taste of leaves is a good complement to fresh tomatoes. Also try the small-leaved bush basil, purple-leaved basil and Greek basil which has a hint of lemon in its taste.

BAY
Evergreen with aromatic leathery leaves which can be used fresh or dried. Be sure to remove leaves from dish before serving as they can be quite painful and even dangerous if ingested.

CHERVIL
Annual. Sow in growing position in mid-spring when weather is warmer. Delicately flavoured; useful with fish and in salads.

Bay tree

CHIVES

Perennial. Onion-flavoured, grass-like leaves invaluable for flavouring dressings and sauces. When cutting, shear the leaves off near to the ground to encourage new growth. Sow seeds in spring and liquid-feed each spring as leaves re-emerge. Other members of the chive family are: the garlic-flavoured chive, the shallot and the tree or Egyptian onion that forms tiny onions at the top of each tall tubular leaf. These are useful for pickling and the leaves can be chopped and used in soups and stews.

DILL

Annual. Sow in midspring. The fresh leaves are marvellous with fish and in salads and sauces, while the fresh seedheads are used for pickling cucumbers. The seed can be gathered and dried for use.

MARJORAM

Shrubby perennial with warm, peppery tasting leaves. There is a golden-leaved variety that makes a pool of bright lemon yellow in the garden and also an annual variety, the knotted marjoram, which has a milder flavour.

Chives

Mint

Marjoram

MINT

Perennial with invasive creeping roots. There is a huge variety to choose from, ranging from the tall-growing broad-leaved Bowles apple-mint to the tiny prostrate pennyroyal with peppermint scented leaves. Eau de Cologne mint smells as its name implies; ginger mint is a golden variegated form that must definitely be grown in a container, as it is so invasive. Have fun experimenting with different types.

PARSLEY

Probably the most popular herb. It is a hardy biennial to treat as an annual. Look for the plain-leaved variety as it has more flavour than the curly leaved type and will also grow continuously for several years as long as it is in a warm sheltered spot. Pick leaves regularly and remove flowerheads as they appear to encourage strong growth.

ROSEMARY

Evergreen shrub and one of the most highly aromatic herbs. Use dried or fresh with meat and in stuffings; try placing a few branches of dried rosemary on the hot charcoal just before putting meat or fish on a barbecue grill. Varieties of rosemary to look for are Miss Jessop's Upright, *Rosmarinus prostratus* (put at the front of raised beds and tubs so it can tumble over the edge), and gilded rosemary which has leaves touched with yellow.

SAGE

Evergreen shrub with felt-textured leaves and a strong flavour. Look for the purple-leaved variety, also the yellow variegated type and *Salvia tricolor* with leaves blotched pink, white and grey-green. Clip over lightly during first year to remove growing tips and encourage bushy growth.

THYME

Evergreen shrub available in a wide variety of leaf form, flavours and habits. The type most used in cooking has small, grey-green leaves and compact, upright habit, but there are lemon-scented varieties, creeping groundcover types, some with yellow or white variegated leaves, others grey and furry. Clip over lightly after flowering.

Sage

Thyme

SHRUBS AND TREES

Trees and shrubs provide the frame for the garden picture, and climbers are the wall on which the picture hangs. They also give privacy and shade to exposed spaces, and provide shelter for underplantings of tender subjects.

Be discerning when choosing which plants to buy; select slow-growing plants with neat habits, and small or dwarf forms, especially if your space is small. Choose evergreen plants with interesting leaf form or colour and ones that have flowers, as the plants will be encouraged to flower abundantly by the restriction of the roots in a container. Make sure that the container you plan to use is large enough; its diameter should be as wide as half the eventual height of the plant.

It is not necessary to list climbers as nearly all are ideal for container gardening. The only thing to remember when choosing them is to avoid the really rampant growers, that would soon fill the tub with roots. The passionflower is one such plant to avoid.

Shrubs
(All evergreen unless indicated otherwise)

Berberis thunbergii. Height up to 50cm (1¾ft). Reddish-green leaves, thorny branches. 'Atropurpurea Nana' is the dwarf form.

Cistus. Height from 60-90cm (2-3ft). Grey-green aromatic foliage, flowers range in colour from white to deep pink, some marked with dark basal blotches. Good on chalk and in hot dry conditions.

Cistus 'Sunset'

Convolvulus cneorum. Height up to 60cm (2ft). Grey-green downy foliage, white flowers.

Daphne odora. 'Aureomarginata' Height to 60cm (ft). Upright spreading habit, leathery leaves edged creamy white. Highly scented flower clusters at the end of each branch in winter and early spring. *D.mezereum* loses its leaves, which are replaced by richly perfumed deep pink flowers covering each branch. Likes acid soil and semi-shade.

Fatsia japonica. Height to 1.5m (5ft). Upright spreading habit, glossy green fan-shaped leaves, umbels of greenish-white flowers.

Lavendula 'Munstead Dwarf'. Height up to 60cm (2ft). Best colour and scent in the lavenders.

Daphne odora

Convolvulus cneorum

Fatsia japonica

44

Lavandula stoechas

Lippia citriodora. Can be pruned into low shrub, trained into standard or grown as climber against wall. Known as lemon-scented verbena, it is deciduous but invaluable for fragrant leaves. Needs warm, sheltered spot or else bring indoors during winter.

Rhododendrons and azaleas. Look for the smaller forms such as *R.yakushimanum*, which has tidy rounded habit and clusters of delicate pink flowers. Also available as small trees. Required acid soil.

Roses (deciduous). Wide variety to choose from, ranging in size from miniatures to tall standards and climbers. Of the old-fashioned shrub roses, choose from the Bourbon and China sections, and the old Hybrid Perpetuals.

Yucca recurvifolia. Height to 1m (3½ft). Long tapering leaves on short stem, dense panicles of sweetly scented ivory coloured flowers in late summer.

Rhododendron 'Baden Baden'

Rosa 'Korp'

Trees

Acer griseum, Paperbark Maple, grows slowly to 5m (16½ft). Cinnamon coloured peeling bark, small leaves tinged red when young. Good autumn colour.

Acer palmatum 'Dissectum Atropurpureum'. Height to 60cm (2ft), weeping mounded habit spreading to 1.2m (3ft 11in). Finely cut reddish purple leaves.

Malus sargentii. Height up to 3m (10ft). Small, scented white flowers in late summer followed by shiny red fruit.

Prunus serrulata – Hybrid Japanese Cherries. Small trees, 5-7m (16½-30ft). Look for 'Amanogawa' – upright habit, clusters of scented pink flowers in late spring; 'Kiku-shidare Sakura' – weeping habit, clear pink flowers in early spring; 'Jo-noi' – neat rounded habit, richly fragrant white flowers in mid-spring.

Acer palmatum (Japanese maple)

Malus sargentii

Acer griseum

Dwarf evergreen fir trees, mainly varieties of *Chamaecyparis lawsoniana, C.obtusa, C.pisifera, Juniperus chinenis, J.media,* and *J.squamata* are invaluable in container gardens. Most garden centres have a wide selection available.

Prunus serrulata 'Shirotae'

nk garden

Thuja orientalis 'Aurea Nana'

INDEX AND ACKNOWLEDGEMENTS

Picture credits
G. Beckett: 33(tr), 35(c), 37(t), 38(t), 43, 44(br), 46(br)
J. Glover: 7(b), 15, 16(t,c), 17(b), 24(t,b), 25(t)
Derek Gould: 8(t), 10, 11(t), 14(tr), 18,22
ICI: 26
David Russell: 28/9, 31(b), 32(b), 35(b), 38(br), 46(t)
Harry Smith Horticultural Photographic Collection: 3, 4/5, 6, 6(t), 8(b), 9, 11(c,b), 12(t,b), 13, 14(tl),
 17(t), 19, 20(t,c,b), 21(b), 23(tl,tr,b), 36(t,b), 37(bl,br), 38(bl), 39, 40, 41(tl,tr,bl), 44(t,bl9,
 45(t,bl,br), 46(bl), 47(tl,tr,b)

Artwork Richard Prideaux & Steve Sandilands